MOTIFS & REPETITIONS
& Other Plays

MOTIFS & REPETITIONS
& Other Plays

C.E. Gatchalian
With a foreword by Bryan Wade

Published by The Writers' Collective
Cranston, Rhode Island

Motifs & Repetitions & Other Plays
By C.E. Gatchalian

An abridged version of the play *Motifs & Repetitions* appeared in the literary anthology *Chasing Halley's Comet*, published by Laughing Willow Books in 1997.

Cover design: Kevin Kwok and Chris MacDonald
Text design: Kevin Kwok
Editing and proofing: Janet Hudgins, A.S. Penne, Scribendi.com
Author photo: Estrella Sauler

ISBN: 1-932133-49-6

Library of Congress Cataloging-in-Publication Data

Gatchalian, C. E., 1974-
Motifs & repetitions & other plays / C.E. Gatchalian ; foreword by Bryan Wade.
     p. cm.
ISBN 1-932133-49-6 (alk. paper)
1. One-act plays, American. I. Title: Motifs and repetitions and other plays. II. Title.
PS3607.A788M68 2003
812'.6—dc21
     2003006650

Printed in the United States of America.

Published by The Writers' Collective
Cranston, Rhode Island

For my mother,
and for Sheck.

ACKNOWLEDGEMENTS:

First and foremost, The New Hogarth Press, for believing in
  me;
Lisa Grant and The Writers' Collective, for making small
  presses like The New Hogarth possible;
Jim Wong-Chu and the Asian Canadian Writers Workshop,
  for giving writers a chance;
my mother, for her unwavering and unending support;
my grandmother, for her gentle tenacity;
Bryan Wade, for his encouragement and generosity;
Brian McGugan, for his artistic brotherhood;
and Sheck MacDonald, for his body and soul.

TABLE OF CONTENTS

Foreword

Theatre, like any other art form, should provoke, transform, entertain, electrify, overwhelm, threaten, disturb, surprise and above all, make you wonder. C.E. Gatchalian's plays do all of the above and more.

Theatre, like any other art form, should create questions in the viewer's mind: why do Adrian and Cathy and Jeff talk directly to us instead of relating to each other (*Motifs & Repetitions*)? Why do three characters have numbers for names and a ten-year-old girl has a name (*Claire*)? Why does Philip sit in a chair with his back to us throughout the play while his wife, Mary, swoops and circles him like a whirlwind? Why does their son, Junior, keep his back to us and never say one word, but only laugh (*Hands*)?

C.E. Gatchalian's plays do all of the above and more. Here are some more questions they create: is this the kind of play where the actors will come into the audience? Why does this remind me of a dream I had the other night? What does it mean? Where is the nearest exit? Why did I laugh at something that normally I never laugh at?

C.E. Gatchalian's writing continues to startle and surprise me. As Peter Birnie, theatre critic for the *Vancouver Sun*, wrote in his review of *Claire*, " *Claire* is evidence of greater, and no doubt even more disturbing, things to come from the writer." I agree wholeheartedly with Mr. Birnie except to say that C.E. Gatchalian's vision as a writer is already highly original, intensely personal, and provocative on many different levels. He has an innate sense of the theatrical in terms of space, rhythm and lighting. His dialogue moves from legato to staccato in the blink of an eye.

Enjoy these plays. They are like jolts of espresso being downloaded into your brain circuitry. They contain scenes of scalding raw emotional power. Yet at the same time there are moments of true compassion and tenderness. C.E. Gatchalian is the real thing. I have no doubt you will be experiencing more plays from this writer in the near future.

Bryan Wade

MOTIFS & REPETITIONS

Motifs & Repetitions was presented at the University of British Columbia's Brave New Playrites Theatre Festival in Vancouver in February 1995, with the following cast:

JEFF   Brian McGugan
CATHY   Christina Schild
ADRIAN   Duncan Shields

Director: Christine Mathieson

It was later adapted into a film produced and directed by Brian McGugan and featuring the above cast. It premiered on Canada's Bravo! channel on April 2, 1997, and later aired on the Knowledge Network as part of the series *Independent Eye* in 1998.

C.E. Gatchalian was one of the winners of the Federation of British Columbia Writers Festival Writing Competition in 1995; *Motifs & Repetitions* was his entry.

CHARACTERS:

JEFF
CATHY
ADRIAN

All in their early twenties, all fairly likeable.

Voices in the dark.

ADRIAN: Jeff.

JEFF: Cathy.

CATHY: Adrian.

Pause.

ADRIAN: Say it.

JEFF: Somebody.

CATHY: Say it.

Pause.

Pools of light on **ADRIAN** *and* **CATHY**. *They are facing the audience.*

CATHY: Adrian?

ADRIAN: Cathy?

CATHY: He's okay.

ADRIAN: She's okay.

CATHY: He's a bit shy.

ADRIAN: She's a bit shy.

CATHY: But he's okay.

ADRIAN: She's okay.

CATHY: It's nothing serious.

ADRIAN: It's nothing serious.

CATHY: I mean we haven't *done* anything.

ADRIAN: I'm not sure she wants me to.

CATHY: Not that I want him to.

ADRIAN: I'm not sure *I* want to.

CATHY: It's not that I love him.

ADRIAN: I can't say I love her.

CATHY: But by now he should've at least *tried* something.

ADRIAN: I don't love anyone.

Beat of darkness.

*Light on **ADRIAN** and **CATHY** together.*

CATHY: Adrian.

ADRIAN: Cathy.

CATHY: Well.

ADRIAN: Well.

CATHY: Nice night.

ADRIAN: What?

CATHY: Nice night.

ADRIAN: It's okay.

Pause.

ADRIAN: About tonight.

CATHY: That's okay.

ADRIAN: I'm sorry.

CATHY: Don't worry about it.

ADRIAN: I'm just really old-fashioned.

CATHY: I understand.

Pause.

ADRIAN: I like your socks.

CATHY: What?

ADRIAN: Your socks.

CATHY: My socks.

ADRIAN: Yeah.

CATHY: You should.

ADRIAN: Yeah?

CATHY: They're from Germany.

ADRIAN: Oh.

CATHY: Straight from Germany.

ADRIAN: Oh.

Pause.

CATHY: Did you like my teacups?

ADRIAN: Your what?

CATHY: Teacups.

ADRIAN: Teacups?

CATHY: Yeah.

ADRIAN: Loved them.

CATHY: Really?

ADRIAN: Truly.

CATHY: Did you like the designs?

ADRIAN: The designs?

CATHY: On the teacups.

ADRIAN: The teacups.

CATHY: Blue and pink flowers with butterflies flying around them.

ADRIAN: Oh, *that.*

CATHY: Yeah, that.

ADRIAN: Yeah.

CATHY: Yeah.

Pause.

ADRIAN: I like your socks.

CATHY: Thanks.

Pause.

ADRIAN: Listen.

CATHY: Yeah?

Pause.

ADRIAN & CATHY: [*Together.*] I wanna call it off.

They laugh awkwardly.

Pause.

ADRIAN & CATHY: [*Together.*] I'm just not ready.

They laugh awkwardly.

Pause.

ADRIAN: About tonight.

CATHY: That's okay.

ADRIAN: I'm sorry.

CATHY: Don't worry about it.

ADRIAN: I'm just really old-fashioned.

CATHY: I understand.

Pause.

ADRIAN: I like your socks.

CATHY: Thanks.

Pause.

ADRIAN: Bye.

CATHY: Bye.

They part. Light lingers on their separate figures.

Beat of darkness.

*Pools of light on **JEFF** and **CATHY**; they are facing the audience.*

JEFF: Cathy?

CATHY: Jeff?

JEFF: What can I say?

CATHY: He's gorgeous.

JEFF: Her hair.

CATHY: His face.

JEFF: [*Getting excited.*] Her breasts.

CATHY: [*Getting excited.*] His chest.

JEFF: Her legs.

CATHY: His butt.

JEFF: And up.

CATHY: And down.

JEFF: [*Comes.*] Oh, God.

CATHY: [*Comes.*] Jesus fuck!

JEFF: What can I say?

CATHY: Nothing much.

JEFF: What's there to say?

CATHY: Nothing much.

JEFF: We don't talk much.

CATHY: It would ruin everything.

JEFF: We're just fucking machines.

CATHY: We're nothing to each other.

JEFF: It's better that way.

CATHY: And I want it that way.

Beat of darkness.

Light on **CATHY** *and* **JEFF,** *locked in a passionate embrace.*

CATHY: Baby.

JEFF: Baby.

CATHY: I've waited all day for this.

JEFF: So have I.

CATHY: God you're gorgeous.

JEFF: So are you.

CATHY: Your face.

JEFF: Your hair.

CATHY: Your chest.

JEFF: Your breasts.

CATHY: Your butt.

JEFF: Your legs.

CATHY: Your—

JEFF: Cathy?

CATHY: What?

JEFF: Shut the fuck up.

CATHY: Huh?

JEFF: Your mouth should be doing something else.

CATHY: Right.

She kneels down and unzips his pants. A knock on the door.

JEFF: Shit.

CATHY: I'll just be a minute.

JEFF: Hurry up.

CATHY: I will.

Light on ADRIAN.

Adrian.

ADRIAN: Cathy.

CATHY: What do you want?

ADRIAN: I just—

CATHY: Yeah?

ADRIAN: Well, I—

CATHY: Yeah?

ADRIAN: [*Noticing JEFF.*] Who's that?

CATHY: Who?

ADRIAN: Jeff?

JEFF: Yo.

ADRIAN: Jeff?

JEFF: Ade.

CATHY: You know each other?

ADRIAN & JEFF: [*Together.*] We're best friends.

CATHY: Jesus fuck.

ADRIAN: [*To JEFF.*] Your fly's open.

JEFF: I know.

ADRIAN: Oh, my God!

CATHY: Jesus fuck.

JEFF: [*To ADRIAN.*] What are you doing here?

ADRIAN: [*Upset.*] I'll never forgive you!

JEFF: Calm down.

ADRIAN: [*Turning to leave.*] I'll never forgive you!

CATHY: [*To ADRIAN.*] Wait.

ADRIAN: What?

CATHY: Jeff.

JEFF: Yo.

CATHY: Could you leave us alone?

JEFF: You and Ade?

CATHY: Please.

JEFF: Hurry up.

CATHY: I will.

JEFF: See you, Ade.

   JEFF leaves light.

ADRIAN: Wow.

CATHY: What?

ADRIAN: You heal fast.

CATHY: What?

ADRIAN: Nothing.

CATHY: What?

ADRIAN: Forget it.

CATHY: Wait.

ADRIAN: What?

CATHY: Why did you come?

ADRIAN: No reason.

CATHY: Bullshit.

ADRIAN: No reason.

CATHY: Bullshit!

Intense silence. They are looking at each other.

ADRIAN: Cathy.

Pause.

CATHY: Yeah?

Pause.

ADRIAN: Nothing.

Pause.

CATHY: Yeah.

Intense silence.

Adrian.

Pause.

ADRIAN: Yeah?

Pause.

CATHY: Nothing.

Pause.

ADRIAN: Yeah.

ADRIAN exits light. JEFF re-enters.

JEFF: Cathy.

CATHY: Jeff.

JEFF: You know him?

CATHY: Who?

JEFF: Ade?

CATHY: Oh.

JEFF: Yeah.

CATHY: We dated.

JEFF: Uh-huh.

CATHY: It was nothing.

JEFF: Uh-huh.

CATHY: It was nothing!

Pause.

JEFF: Are you all right?

CATHY: I will be.

JEFF: Yeah?

CATHY: If you fuck me.

Beat of darkness.

Pools of light on JEFF and CATHY; they are facing the audience.

JEFF: Fuck.

CATHY: Fuck.

JEFF: That's all we ever do.

CATHY: And that's all I want.

JEFF: That's all I ever promised her.

CATHY: And that's all I ever wanted.

JEFF: I'm seeing other girls.

CATHY: Who cares if he does?

JEFF: So what? I don't love her.

CATHY: He's nothing to me.

JEFF: We're just fucking machines.

CATHY: We're nothing to each other.

JEFF: I don't believe in love.

CATHY: There's no such thing.

JEFF: I don't love anyone.

CATHY: And I never will.

Beat of darkness.

Light on **JEFF** *and* **CATHY** *in the middle of a vicious fight.*

JEFF: Why the fuck are you so upset?

CATHY: I'm not talking to you!

JEFF: Just hear me out for Chrissake! I never committed to you and you never committed to me. I told you I was seeing other girls and you said it was okay!

CATHY: [*Singing.*] "My bonny lies over the ocean, my bonny lies over the sea, my bonny lies over the ocean, oh, bring back my bonny to me."

CATHY: Go ahead. Fuck those floozies.

JEFF: Cathy.

CATHY: But not while I'm looking!

27

JEFF: [*Grabbing her.*] Cathy!

CATHY: Let go!

JEFF: You're a fucking turn-off, you know that?

CATHY spits in his face. He stops just short of hitting her.

Pause.

JEFF: [*Hugging her.*] I'm sorry …   **CATHY:** Let go of me, you
I'm sorry … I'm sorry …   bastard! Let go of me!

CATHY starts to cry.

Pause.

They look at each other.

Intense silence.

JEFF: Cathy.

Pause.

CATHY: Yeah?

Pause.

JEFF: Nothing.

Pause.

CATHY: Yeah.

Intense silence. JEFF turns to leave.

Jeff.

Pause.

JEFF: Yeah?

Pause.

CATHY: Nothing.

Pause.

JEFF: Yeah.

JEFF exits. Light lingers on **CATHY.**

Beat of darkness.

Pools of light on **ADRIAN, JEFF,** *and* **CATHY;** *all are facing the audience.*

ADRIAN: I can't think straight.

JEFF: I can't work.

CATHY: I can't sleep.

ADRIAN: I can't eat.

CATHY: All I do is eat.

ADRIAN: I feel sick.

CATHY: All I do is puke.

ADRIAN: I can't think straight.

JEFF: This throbbing headache.

CATHY: All I think is Jeff.

JEFF: All I think is Cathy.

CATHY: All I think is Adrian.

JEFF: Cathy.

ADRIAN: Jeff.

CATHY: Adrian.

ADRIAN: Cathy.

JEFF: This throbbing headache.

ADRIAN: This thing burning inside me.

CATHY: It's like a fever.

ADRIAN: It's burning me up.

JEFF: It's making me sick.

CATHY: It's making me puke.

ADRIAN: Who asked you?

JEFF: Who asked you?

CATHY: Who the fuck asked you?

ADRIAN: Swallow it.

JEFF: Swallow it.

CATHY: Swallow your fucking pride.

JEFF: I need you.

ADRIAN: I need you.

CATHY: Both of you.

ADRIAN: Both of you.

CATHY: Jeff.

JEFF: Cathy.

CATHY: Adrian.

ADRIAN: Help me!

Beat of darkness.

Pools of light on **ADRIAN** *and* **JEFF***, facing the audience.*

JEFF: Adrian?

ADRIAN: Jeff?

JEFF: Ade's a nice guy.

ADRIAN: Jeff.

JEFF: We've known each other since first grade.

ADRIAN: Jeff.

JEFF: He was a bit of a sissy.

ADRIAN: Jeff.

JEFF: But I liked him.

ADRIAN: Jeff.

JEFF: I was his bodyguard in school.

ADRIAN: Jeff.

JEFF: Fought off all the bullies who wanted to hurt him.

ADRIAN: Jeff.

JEFF: And he's had a soft spot for me ever since.

ADRIAN: Jeff.

JEFF: He was really angry when he found out I was dating Cathy.

ADRIAN: Jeff.

JEFF: But when we broke up, Ade forgave me.

ADRIAN: Jeff.

JEFF: I like Ade.

ADRIAN: Jeff.

JEFF: He's a swell guy.

ADRIAN: Oh, Jeff.

Beat of darkness.

Light on ADRIAN and JEFF together.

JEFF: Hey, man.

ADRIAN: Hey.

JEFF: How's life?

ADRIAN: Not bad.

Pause.

ADRIAN: I'm sorry.

JEFF: About what?

ADRIAN: Things.

JEFF: What things?

ADRIAN: You and Cathy.

JEFF: Will you get off it?

ADRIAN: What?

JEFF: That's all you ever talk about.

ADRIAN: But I *am* sorry.

JEFF: It's no big deal.

ADRIAN: I'm sorry.

JEFF: Just forget about it.

Pause.

ADRIAN: Jeff.

JEFF: What?

ADRIAN: Got a cigarette?

JEFF: Sure.

ADRIAN: Thanks.

JEFF: Let me light it for you.

ADRIAN: Thanks.

JEFF lights it.

Pause.

Jeff.

JEFF: What?

ADRIAN: I like your socks.

JEFF: What?

ADRIAN: Your socks.

JEFF: My socks?

ADRIAN: Yeah.

JEFF: Thanks.

Pause.

ADRIAN: Jeff?

JEFF: What?

ADRIAN: Can I talk to you about something?

JEFF: Sure big guy. What?

Intense silence.

ADRIAN: Jeff.

Intense silence.

JEFF: Don't.

Intense silence.

ADRIAN: Jeff, please.

JEFF: [*Scared.*] No!

ADRIAN: I have to say it.

JEFF: Get the fuck away from me!

JEFF exits the light.

ADRIAN: JEFF!

Blackout.

3 count.

*Light on **JEFF** and **CATHY**. They are facing the audience. A clock ticks in the background.*

CATHY: It is ten minutes to two. Early Sunday morning.

JEFF: I can't sleep.

CATHY: I can't sleep.

JEFF: I've missed two weeks of work.

CATHY: This headache is killing me.

JEFF: And it won't go away.

CATHY: It's like a fever, I tell you.

JEFF: Throbbing.

CATHY: Burning.

JEFF: No girl should mean this much.

CATHY: Why didn't I just say it?

JEFF: Christ, what about Ade?

CATHY: I didn't have the guts.

JEFF: He's my best friend.

CATHY: God, I have to say it.

JEFF: Fuck, I have to say it.

CATHY: Jeff.

JEFF: Cathy.

CATHY & JEFF: [*Together.*] Adrian.

*Light on **ADRIAN**.*

ADRIAN: I like your socks.

Beat of darkness.

34

Lights on JEFF and CATHY. The clock continues to tick. Accelerando. Crescendo.

JEFF: It is five minutes to two. Early Sunday morning.

CATHY: Jeff.

JEFF: I'm gonna phone him.

CATHY: Adrian.

JEFF: I owe him that.

CATHY: Somebody.

JEFF: But he'll think I'm a fag.

CATHY: Just say it.

JEFF: I'm going over to Cathy's.

Light on ADRIAN.

ADRIAN: I'm just really old-fashioned.

JEFF: Right now.

CATHY: I wish I'd never met you.

ADRIAN: I like your socks.

JEFF: I'm here.

CATHY: Fuck both of you.

ADRIAN: I like your teacups.

JEFF: I'm gonna tell her.

CATHY: You make me puke.

ADRIAN: I like the designs.

JEFF: Knock.

CATHY: I'm so lonely.

ADRIAN: The flowers.

35

JEFF: Just knock.

CATHY: I'm so lonely.

ADRIAN: The butterflies.

JEFF: I can't.

CATHY: I'm so fucking lonely.

ADRIAN: The vomit.

JEFF: You've got no guts.

CATHY: Just say it.

ADRIAN: I'm just really old-fashioned.

JEFF: Who asked you?

CATHY: Who asked you?

ADRIAN: Who the fuck asked you?

JEFF: Swallow it.

CATHY: Swallow it.

ADRIAN: Swallow your fucking pride.

JEFF: I need you.

ADRIAN: I need you.

CATHY: Both of you.

ADRIAN: Both of you.

CATHY: Jeff.

ADRIAN: Oh, Jeff.

JEFF: Cathy.

ADRIAN: Oh, Cathy.

CATHY: Adrian.

JEFF: Hey, big guy!

CATHY: Say it!

ADRIAN: Both of you!

JEFF: I can't!

Lights out on JEFF and CATHY; ADRIAN alone.

ADRIAN: I like your socks.

Pause.

Lights back on JEFF and CATHY. The clock ticks loudly. Presto. Orgasmic.

CATHY: JEFF!

ADRIAN: I WANT YOU!

JEFF: CATHY!

ADRIAN: I WANT YOU!

CATHY: ADRIAN!

JEFF: HEY BIG GUY!

CATHY: SAY IT!

ADRIAN: BOTH OF YOU!

JEFF: I CAN'T!

Lights out on JEFF and CATHY; ADRIAN alone.

ADRIAN: I ... LIKE ... YOUR ... SOCKS ...

Pause.

Blackout.

Sound of glass shattering; the voices of ADRIAN and CATHY in the dark.

CATHY: Who's there?

ADRIAN: Shut up!

CATHY: Adrian!

ADRIAN: [*Pinning CATHY's arms behind her.*] SHUT UP!

CATHY: [*Struggling.*] NO ... NO ... NO!

The clock strikes two.

Silence: 5 count.

CATHY's *sobbing voice in the dark. She is singing very slowly.*

"Bring back, bring back,
Oh, bring back my bonny to me, to me;
Bring back, bring back,
Oh, bring back my bonny to me."

Silence.

Pools of light on each character. All are facing the audience; all are downtrodden. The pace is very slow.

ADRIAN: Jeff.

JEFF: Cathy.

CATHY: Adrian.

Pause.

ADRIAN: Say it.

JEFF: Somebody.

CATHY: Say it.

Pause.

ADRIAN: I love you.

Pause.

JEFF: I love you.

Pause.

CATHY: I love you.

Tableau. Fade out. The end.

HANDS

Hands was given a staged reading at the Asian Heritage Month festival in Vancouver in May 1998, with the following cast:

MARY   Janet Glassford
PHILIP   John R. Taylor
JUNIOR   Jun Obayashi

Director: C.E. Gatchalian

Hands was short-listed for the Playwriting Award at the 1996 Pacific Northwest Writers Conference Literary Contest.

CHARACTERS:

MARY, 49
PHILIP, 51
JUNIOR, 23

SCENERY:

Extremely simple. A chair (stage right, occupied by **PHILIP**; a table with a vase of azaleas; bare, white walls.

MARY is free to use all the space the director deems necessary.

JUNIOR's playing space is stage left.

Lights up. **MARY** *is centre stage.* **PHILIP** *is seated in a chair, stage right, reading a newspaper, his back to the audience.*

MARY: Philip.

Pause.

PHILIP: Mary.

Pause.

MARY: Happy anniversary, Philip.

Pause.

PHILIP: What?

MARY: Happy anniversary.

PHILIP: Why do you say it that way?

MARY: What way?

PHILIP: As if you thought I'd forgotten.

MARY: What are you talking about?

PHILIP: I didn't forget.

MARY: I didn't think you did.

PHILIP: I did not forget.

MARY: Did I say you did?

Pause.

Philip.

PHILIP: Mary.

MARY: Guess who I ran into the other day.

PHILIP: Anne Barrie.

MARY: How did you know?

PHILIP: I just guessed.

MARY: Guessed?

PHILIP: Yes.

MARY: Yes. I saw Anne Barrie the other day. It's been aeons since I last saw her. She invited me to her house and we had a long, wonderful chat. She's as radiant as ever.

PHILIP: Yes.

MARY: The kids are off to college. John Junior's engaged to be married.

PHILIP: And John?

MARY: Engaged to be married.

PHILIP: Senior.

MARY: Senior?

PHILIP: Yes.

MARY: I don't know. He wasn't there.

PHILIP: Oh.

MARY: No. But Anne was as radiant as ever. They've redecorated the house since the last time we visited. Anne told me she was so sick of that house that after the kids moved out she wanted to sell it. But John refused, and after ferocious debate she agreed to stay as long as they could redecorate it. Oh, Philip, you should have seen their new wallpaper. The most gorgeous floral design I'd ever seen.

PHILIP: Yes.

MARY: A flurry of azaleas on a burgundy backdrop.

PHILIP: Yes.

MARY: I thought it was wonderful. It made the house seem warm.

PHILIP: It made the house seem dark.

MARY: You weren't there. How would you know?

PHILIP: Because I know. I just know.

MARY: It made it warm.

PHILIP: Dark.

MARY: Warm!

Pause.

It made it warm.

Pause.

As a matter of fact I'd like to get the same kind of wallpaper myself.

PHILIP: [*Firmly.*] You will do no such thing. I like the walls bare. White.

MARY: Yes, Philip.

PHILIP: Simplicity.

MARY: Yes, Philip.

Pause.

Anne was as radiant as ever.

PHILIP: Yes.

Pause.

MARY: Philip.

Pause.

PHILIP: I didn't forget.

MARY: Forget what?

PHILIP: Our anniversary.

MARY: I never said you did.

PHILIP: I am not a stupid man.

MARY: I never said you were.

Pause.

You should have seen Anne Barrie's kitchen. It was as clean and spotless as ever. So clean you could practically eat breakfast off it.

PHILIP: Yes, Mary.

MARY: Anne is an incredible homemaker.

PHILIP: Not unlike yourself, Mary.

MARY: Do you think so?

PHILIP: Yes, Mary.

MARY: You're not just saying that.

PHILIP: No, Mary.

MARY: I try, my darling.

PHILIP: Yes, Mary.

MARY: I *do* try.

PHILIP: Yes, Mary.

MARY: But it's so difficult sometimes.

PHILIP: I know, Mary.

MARY: But I *do* try.

PHILIP: Yes, Mary.

MARY: Please believe me.

PHILIP: Yes, Mary.

Pause.

MARY: Philip.

PHILIP: Yes.

MARY: Give me your hand.

PHILIP: My what?

MARY: Your hand, darling. Your hand.

She takes his hand, caresses it, kisses it.

This may surprise you, but it was your hands that first attracted me to you.

PHILIP: Really.

MARY: We shook hands. It was so strong, your handshake, so certain. I knew after that that I didn't want to be with anyone else.

Pause.

Philip.

PHILIP: Yes.

MARY: About the wallpaper.

PHILIP: There will be no wallpaper.

MARY: But Philip—

PHILIP: I like the walls bare.

MARY: Yes.

PHILIP: White.

MARY: Yes.

Pause.

Philip.

PHILIP: Yes.

MARY: Put your paper down.

PHILIP: What?

MARY: [*With some anger.*] Put your paper down.

PHILIP: I don't think I will.

Pause.

MARY snatches paper from PHILIP, crumples it, hurls it across the room.

MARY: Guess what I found.

PHILIP: I don't appreciate your doing that.

MARY: GUESS WHAT I FOUND.

PHILIP: HOW DARE YOU DO THAT.

MARY: Guess what I found in the basement this morning.

From her skirt pocket she withdraws a pair of mittens.

Junior's mittens. You remember, don't you? The mittens I made for him for his sixth birthday. Or was it Christmas? Yes, it was Christmas. Yes. His birthday and Christmas are only a month apart—that's why I keep getting them mixed up. It was the year we first discovered his incredible talent, remember? The year that professor at the academy declared him a prodigy. So I simply had to make him new mittens, to protect those hands of his from the cold. He has beautiful hands. He has *beautiful* hands.

PHILIP: Has?

MARY: Yes.

PHILIP: The present tense?

Pause.

MARY: Let's not get into this.

PHILIP: We agreed never to speak of him in the present tense.

MARY: Let's not get into this.

PHILIP: He *had* beautiful hands.

MARY: Let's just forget it, all right?

PHILIP: HE *HAD* BEAUTIFUL HANDS.

Pause.

[*Calmly.*] He *had* beautiful hands, just like his father—that is until his mother pushed him into piano lessons and made moth wings out of them.

MARY: He had talent!

PHILIP: His hands were never meant to unfold! [*He raises his fist.*] His hands were never meant to unfold. But they did. Just like that [*on "that" he snaps his fingers*]. And he proved himself incompetent.

MARY: He is not incompetent.

PHILIP: Is?

MARY: He is a prodigy.

PHILIP: Is?

MARY: He is our son.

PHILIP: Is?

Beat.

Is? Is? Is?

Pause.

Shut up if you insist on speaking of him in the present tense.

Silence.

MARY: Anne Barrie … she's such an expert homemaker.

PHILIP: Not unlike yourself, Mary.

MARY: Do you think so?

PHILIP: Yes, Mary.

MARY: You're not just saying that?

PHILIP: No, Mary.

MARY: I do try. Really, I do try.

PHILIP: Yes, Mary.

MARY: [*On the verge of tears, hugging him.*] I *do* try, my darling. Please believe me.

PHILIP: Yes, Mary.

MARY: Please believe me!

Silence.

PHILIP: So you like my hands, do you?

MARY: Very much, Philip.

PHILIP: I'm not the least bit surprised. I like them myself.

MARY: They're so strong.

PHILIP: Yes.

MARY: They have a certain … rough beauty.

Pause.

PHILIP: I was a boy. A very bad boy. Every time I pulled a stunt my father would have me hold my hand out and he'd take a whip to it, five strikes of the whip—one, two, three, four, five—five strikes of the whip and nothing else, just the whip my great-grandfather had left my grandfather had left my father. And you know what? It thrilled me. I was mesmerized by the rhythm, the rhythm of it all, the motion, the controlled motion of his hand—he had beautiful hands—the curve of that whip falling flat on my palm, the blue vein of determination popping out between his brows, the sweat oozing from his temples, the glorious glow in his beautiful eyes. I needed it, I knew I needed it, despite the pain, oh the pain, but it was necessary. It was right. And it gave me a thrill.

MARY: A thrill?

PHILIP: It was all…for the sake of…simplicity.

Pause.

Could you retrieve my paper, please?

MARY: Of course, Philip.

*She picks up the paper, irons it out, gives it to **PHILIP**.*

Pause.

Philip.

PHILIP: [*Reading the paper again.*] What?

MARY: [*Hesitantly.*] Aren't you tired of this house?

PHILIP: [*Putting the paper down.*] What?

MARY: This house. Aren't you tired of it?

PHILIP: Why do you ask that?

MARY: Please don't be angry …

PHILIP: … how dare you even suggest that …

MARY: … but it's been something I've been meaning to ask you …

PHILIP: HOW DARE YOU ASK THAT.

MARY: Please, darling, just listen to me.

PHILIP: We've lived in this house for twenty-five years and I have no intention of ever leaving it. Is that clear?

MARY: Philip, please—

PHILIP: IS THAT CLEAR?

Pause.

***PHILIP** returns to his newspaper.*

MARY: [*A tremor in her voice.*] Philip?

PHILIP: What?

MARY: There is something I must tell you, something I've been meaning to tell you for quite a while now, but I haven't had the courage, and you haven't had the time.

Pause.

I … I think we have to do something about this house. Every morning I sit in this room, my hands folded in my lap, and I see this table, this vase of azaleas, these chairs, these walls. I will sit here motionless for hours on end, trying to see more than what is here. But I can't. I can't live like this, darling—it's tearing me apart. One day you'll walk in on me and I'll be cutting my skin open with the broken pieces of this vase.

Pause.

She turns to **PHILIP.**

Have you been listening to me?

PHILIP: I never listen to you when you talk nonsense.

Pause.

MARY *kneels before him.*

MARY: Philip, have you no compassion, no compassion for me at all? Please try to understand. If we don't do something—paper the walls, what have you—I don't know what's going to happen, I swear I don't know what I'll do to myself. So for my sake, for our sake: compassion, Philip, compassion!

PHILIP: If you want to leave me, Mary, no one's stopping you.

Pause.

If you hate this house so much, just leave.

Pause.

Go on.

Pause.

[*Angrier.*] LEAVE!

Silence.

MARY rises, laughs a helpless laugh.

Pause.

Talking as if simply for the hell of it, she again takes mittens out of skirt pocket.

MARY: These mittens. They were Junior's, remember? I found them while I was rummaging in the basement this morning. Christmas, wasn't it? Yes, Christmas, of course, Christmas. I gave them to him when he was six years old. How small his hands were. How big they are now.

PHILIP: Are?

Pause.

MARY: Yes.

Pause.

PHILIP: Why do you use the present tense?

Pause.

MARY: [*Hesitantly, but with some defiance.*] Because … I want to.

PHILIP: I thought we agreed never to speak of him in the present tense.

MARY: I think I've forgotten the exact reason why we shouldn't.

PHILIP: Well, perhaps I should remind you.

MARY: Well, perhaps you should.

Pause.

PHILIP: He failed us, Mary …

MARY: He has not failed us …

PHILIP: … he nearly brought this house down …

MARY: … you're just imagining things …

PHILIP: … he wanted to bring this house down …

MARY: … this is absolute nonsense …

PHILIP: … but you know what? He didn't! He couldn't! I saved our souls and I saved this house from the rage of that disgusting pervert.

MARY: Anne Barrie is as radiant as ever. She redid the walls—did I tell you that? With the most gorgeous floral design I've ever seen.

Pause.

MARY: I think wallpaper would do wonders for our house, don't you?

PHILIP: I saved this house, Mary, and don't you forget it.

MARY: Our walls have been bare for too long now, don't you think?

PHILIP: I stood my ground. I saved us both.

MARY: They're practically screaming for cover.

PHILIP: He's dead.

MARY: We're going to get exactly the same kind of wallpaper the Barries have.

PHILIP: He's dead.

MARY: I'll start first thing in the morning.

PHILIP: He's dead.

MARY: I'm going to the kitchen.

PHILIP: You're not going anywhere.

MARY: I have to make you coffee.

PHILIP: You wanted to talk about him and that's exactly what we're going to do.

MARY: Philip, please—

PHILIP: He's dead.

MARY: He's *not* dead.

PHILIP: He *is* dead.

MARY: He is *not* dead!

PHILIP: But we must go on living as if he were.

MARY: He is *not* dead! He's coming home this afternoon!

Pause.

PHILIP: He is *not* coming home.

MARY: Philip, he is.

PHILIP: You're lying!

MARY: I'm not lying!

PHILIP: [*In absolute terror.*] HE IS *NOT* COMING HOME! HE IS *NOT* COMING HOME!

Pause.

PHILIP *takes a deep breath, clears his throat, regains his composure.*

PHILIP: Why … why would he come home, after all that's happened?

MARY: What's happened?

PHILIP: Oh, Mary, you really are testing my patience today, you know that?

MARY: I haven't the slightest idea what you're talking about.

Silence.

PHILIP: Our child … our only child … is a degenerate.

Silence.

MARY: He is not … that.

Pause.

PHILIP: Oh, Mary, he told us right to our face.

Pause.

MARY: It was a lie! It was just a silly story he made up!

Pause.

PHILIP: Mary, get this straight: he's dead.

MARY: No!

PHILIP: He died the day he walked out that door! And nothing will ever change that.

Silence.

PHILIP returns to newspaper. **MARY,** *visibly shaken, begins to speak tremulously.*

MARY: Guess who I ran into the other day.

PHILIP: Anne Barrie.

MARY: How did you know?

PHILIP: I just guessed.

MARY: Anne was as radiant as ever. John Jr.'s engaged to be married.

PHILIP: And John?

MARY: Engaged to be married.

PHILIP: Senior.

MARY: Senior.

PHILIP: Yes.

MARY: Oh.

Pause.

I didn't see him. He wasn't there.

PHILIP: He wasn't there.

MARY: No.

PHILIP: It *has* been a long time since we last saw them, hasn't it?

MARY: Yes.

PHILIP: The four of us used to be so close.

MARY: Yes.

PHILIP: We used to spend all our weekends with them.

MARY: Yes.

PHILIP: They'd come to our place or we'd go to theirs.

MARY: Yes.

PHILIP: But for some reason we just drifted apart.

MARY: Yes.

PHILIP: They stopped calling us and we stopped calling them.

MARY: Yes.

PHILIP: It's too bad. I'm beginning to miss them.

Pause.

It *has* been a long time since we last saw them.

MARY: Yes.

PHILIP: I've known John since I was a kid.

MARY: Yes.

PHILIP: I think he was always very fond of you.

MARY: Was he?

PHILIP: I was never really sure what you thought of him.

MARY: Not much.

PHILIP: Not much?

MARY: I never cared for him.

PHILIP: No?

MARY: No.

Pause.

PHILIP: The four of us used to be so close.

MARY: Yes.

PHILIP: All those weekends we spent with them.

MARY: Yes.

PHILIP: All the fun things we did with them.

MARY: Yes.

PHILIP: Camping.

MARY: Yes.

PHILIP: Eating.

MARY: Yes.

PHILIP: Swinging.

Pause.

MARY: What?

PHILIP: Oh, yes. That's right. I forgot.

Pause.

I took a rain check. I think Anne's a dog.

Intense silence.

MARY: [*Nervously, turning to leave.*] I really must make your coffee now.

Pause.

MARY *does not leave.*

PHILIP: Mary. Really. There's no use hiding. It's all out in the open now.

Pause.

MARY *trembles, begins to cry.*

PHILIP: [*Slowly, very calmly.*] Oh, Mary, really. There's no use crying. I knew about you and John a long time ago. Believe me, I understand. These things happen. I saw the two of you fucking but I took it in stride. Really, Mary, you must stop crying. Because no matter what you do, nothing will ever change. Our house will remain as it is.

Pause.

PHILIP *returns to his newspaper.* **MARY** *is trembling, in tears.*

MARY: Philip.

PHILIP: Mary.

MARY: John and I called it off a long time ago.

PHILIP: Really, Mary, there's no need to explain.

MARY: I never meant to hurt you.

PHILIP: Of course not.

MARY: Please forgive me.

PHILIP: I already have.

MARY: [*Kneeling before him.*] I never meant to—

PHILIP: Be quiet.

MARY: But Philip—

PHILIP: BE QUIET!

Pause.

[Very *calmly*.] I'm on the edge, Mary. *Just* on the edge. I'm fifty-one years old, and I've learned to believe what I want to believe. Right now I'm making myself believe that you're the girl I married twenty-five years ago, not the haggard old baggage that you are now. But I'm also prepared to forget about your little thing with John Barrie, and simply chuckle at the idea of any man not fully off his rocker even thinking of having an affair with you. But I *am* on the edge, Mary— *just* on the edge. So either you shut the fuck up right here and now or I'll drag you by the hair to the garage and blow your brains out. Really, Mary, it's up to you.

Silence.

MARY: [*Slowly rising.*] Oh, Philip ...

Pause.

What is happening?

Pause.

What in hell on earth is happening?

The doorbell rings.

Junior?

Pause.

Junior?

*Lights suddenly up on **JUNIOR**, stage left, his back to the audience. He is wearing a black leather jacket and pants, an earring, dark glasses. His head is shaved.*

Junior.

MARY goes to him, hugs him.

You're a bit early, aren't you?

62

He is very still, does not respond.

Philip?

She goes to **PHILIP**.

PHILIP?

Silence.

PHILIP *tosses his head and resumes reading the paper; for the rest of the play, save the bit at the end, he is completely incommunicado.* **MARY** *returns to* **JUNIOR**.

Don't mind him, dear. He's just tired is all. He spent the whole morning putting up new wallpaper. The living room isn't done yet. Just the bedroom.

Pause.

How are you?

Pause.

[*Tenderly.*] I missed you.

Pause.

You've … changed so much … hasn't he,
Philip?

She forces a laugh.

Let me see your hands.

She takes them, kisses them.

Oh, how strong they are! But then they've got to be strong—you're a concert pianist, for God's sake! And your father here calls your hands moth wings!

Pause.

Guess what I found.

She withdraws mittens from skirt pocket.

Your old mittens. Remember? I gave them to you for
Christmas when you were six years old. How small your
hands were. How big they are now.

Pause.

I made them for you the year that professor at the Academy
declared you a prodigy. I simply had to make you new
mittens, to protect these hands of yours from the cold. And
you loved these mittens so much that you wore them all the
time, even in the summertime. "I am a concert pianist,"
you'd tell those horrid boys next door. "I have to protect my
hands." And they'd beat you up black and blue and you'd
run to me crying, and I'd take you in my arms and tell you
that everything would be all right, that when you grew up
you'd stand head and shoulders above them all.

Pause.

How quiet you are today. But then you've always been
quiet, haven't you? You never did say much, did you?
Except with your beautiful, beautiful eyes.

Pause.

Why do you hide your eyes under such dark, dark glasses?
Take them off. Please? For me?

He does not.

Pause.

I guess you're wondering how your father and I have been
doing.

Beat.

We've been doing fine. Haven't we, Philip? Whatever
problems we may have had we've worked through and
taken care of. That's because we believe in each other, and
we believe in the life we've built together. Every morning I
sit in this room, my hands folded in my lap, and I see this
table, this vase of azaleas, these chairs, these walls. And I
will sit here motionless for hours on end, thanking God for
giving us the life we have.

Pause.

We wake up.

Beat.

We eat breakfast.

Beat.

Your father goes to work.

Beat.

I clean the house.

Beat.

Your father comes home.

Beat.

We eat dinner.

Beat.

We watch some TV.

Beat.

We go to bed.

Beat.

The simplicity of it all. And we love it.

Pause.

Every day when the time is right I'll take his hand in mine. It's so strong, his hand, so certain. I'm the luckiest woman in the world.

Pause.

MARY's eyes catch JUNIOR's, falter.

Why do you look at me that way? Stop it. [*Angrily.*] Stop it, do you hear me? I won't have it!

She glares at him, then abruptly turns away.

You're so smug. You think you've got everything figured out, don't you! Well let me tell you something: things aren't the way you think they are. We love this table, this vase of azaleas, these chairs, these walls. We love this house! And we love each other! We are happy! WE ARE HAPPY!

Pause.

JUNIOR *is shaking his head.*

Is this what you came home for? To disrespect us? Is it?

She laughs bitterly.

Your father was right about you all a—

She stops herself, takes a deep breath, regains her composure.

My dear, can't you show me a little respect? Please?

Silence.

Guess what I found. Your old mittens, remember? I gave them to you for—

She stops herself.

I showed them to you already, didn't I?

Silence.

How's your music going? I read reviews of your performance with the symphony the other day. They were rapturous, of course. I'm so proud of you.

Pause.

You do … wear a suit … when you perform, don't you? You look so much better in a suit. You really do.

Pause.

It's your father's and my anniversary today. But of course you knew that, didn't you? And no dear, he didn't forget. Your father did *not* forget. I know you'd like to think that he did but he didn't. He did *not* forget. In fact he gave me the most wonderful present he's ever given me. Wallpaper. A flurry of azaleas on a burgundy backdrop. The living room isn't done yet. Just the bedroom.

Pause.

[*Abruptly.*] All right, he hasn't put up any wallpaper, as if I can ever expect this S.O.B. to allow so much as a gob of spit to liven up this house.

JUNIOR laughs.

Don't laugh at me! Don't! Don't laugh at me!

JUNIOR continues to laugh.

You really are having a ball, aren't you! You had this all planned before you came, didn't you! Let's have a little fun and peeve poor Mommy. Well, look at me. Look at me! Do I … look … peeved?

She looks peeved.

Pause.

Why did you come home? Why on earth did you come home?

Pause.

She catches herself.

[*Quieter.*] Oh, yes. I forgot. I invited you, didn't I?

Pause.

I invited you home … because I want you to right … a wrong.

Pause.

What you said about yourself … when you left this house … that was a lie. Wasn't it? Wasn't it?

Pause.

You hated this house. You wanted to be thrown out. That's why you made up that silly story about yourself.

She kneels before him.

But things will be different now. I promise you. They will!

She takes his hands, kisses them.

JUNIOR … JUNIOR … such strong, beautiful hands! I want you to come home! We need you back in our lives!

She hugs his legs desperately.

You hurt us so much with that lie—that terrible, terrible lie—but we forgive you. We forgive you … because we love you.

She hugs him again.

Pause.

It *was* … just a lie … wasn't it?

Pause.

Answer me.

Silence.

Speak!

JUNIOR begins to laugh. MARY rises, stares incredulously at him.

What are you laughing at?

Pause.

What are you laughing at?

Pause.

Philip? Philip? What is he laughing at?

JUNIOR continues to laugh.

Stop it!

Beat.

Stop it!

Beat.

Philip? Philip? Tell him to stop it!

JUNIOR continues to laugh.

Is it true?

Beat.

Is it true?

Beat.

Answer me!

Beat.

Speak!

JUNIOR continues to laugh. MARY is shaking violently.

Is it true?

Beat.

Is it true?

Pause.

[*Sobbing.*] Oh, God … please God … no …

She runs to PHILIP, clutches him.

Philip? Tell me it's not true! PHILIP? TELL ME IT'S NOT TRUE!

PHILIP is completely still, does not respond. MARY lets go of JUNIOR, rises.

This is *not* how it's supposed to be! This is *not* how it's supposed to be! [*To JUNIOR, seethingly.*] So you *do* want to destroy us! You *do* want to bring us down! [*Crescendoing.*] Well it won't work. You know why? Because you're dead.

69

YOU'RE DEAD! Glory be to God in heaven you're dead! YOU'RE DEAD! [*Apoplectic.*] There's nothing I hate more than having a pervert's corpse in my house! So get out of my house! GET OUT!

She draws her hand back, almost slaps him but doesn't. **JUNIOR** *stops laughing. They are both very still. Weeping, he moves away from her. She goes to him, touches him.*

[*Contritely.*] I'm sorry.

Pause.

I'm sorry.

Pause.

I couldn't help it.

Pause.

You hurt me.

Silence.

She moves away from him.

You're not dead … you can never be dead … you're here … even when you're not here.

Pause.

When I look at you now, when I look at what you've … become … it makes me wonder why I ever tried, why I ever bothered … pretending. [*She laughs bitterly.*] When I look at you now, when I look at what you've … become … this table, this vase of azaleas, these chairs, these walls … amount to nothing. Absolutely nothing. [*Pause. More to herself.*] The filth sweeps in … through the cracks in these walls … the grudges, the lies, the secrets … things you say in the heat of anger which you say you don't mean but do, the silences between the words, the things you hide your eyes behind, the hands you caress but which refuse to caress back … and the little things: the socks you forget to clean, the tiles in the bathroom you forget to scrub, the earrings you drop in some dingy motel room while your husband's best friend is busy swallowing your neck. [*To JUNIOR.*] And you ... *you* ... so self-righteous and smug, mocking us, laughing at us, thinking you're so much better than us, untouched by the filth because you managed to get out. Well, I've got news for you: you didn't get out! You'll never get out! The reason you're what you are is because of us. *Us!* And you'll wear that scar for the rest of your life.

Silence.

Just because you got out ... or think you got out ... doesn't mean the rest of us want to. [*Beat.*] Did it ever occur to you that there are other things beyond one's own self-centered existence? Can't you show a little—respect—for those of us who've persevered, who've carried on with what's right ... and what's normal?

Pause.

She looks at him intently, her eyes falter.

Don't look at me like that! I won't have it!

She turns quickly away.

You're no better than we are ... you're no better than we are ... judging us, thinking you're so much better than us. Because deep down, deep down, you're nowhere near as secure as you think you are. Deep down, you're a mess ... just like we are.

Silence.

She darts her eyes from JUNIOR to PHILIP and back.

[*As if simply for the hell of it.*] I read your reviews with the symphony the other day, they were rapturous, of course, I'm so proud of you.

Silence.

[*To JUNIOR but looking intently at PHILIP.*] Your father wants you dead. He wants to think that you're dead. I never understood why, but I think I do now.

Pause.

When we see this table, this vase of azaleas, these chairs, these walls, what we see ... is death. Not the epic whittling away of the body—the way it often is for people like you—but another kind of death, one that's beautiful and right, that click that turns everything pure white. The world's crystal clear when you're dead. It makes you wonder why you were ever alive.

Pause.

Your father is dead. And I suppose so am I. And he wants you dead ... he wants to think that you're dead. If he doesn't, then we're ... alive ... and this ... simplicity ... will end.

Pause.

She goes to **PHILIP.**

Your father doesn't hate you ... he really doesn't hate you. In some strange way I think he admires you.

Pause.

But he wants you dead, so that we can be dead. So go away ... please ... and let us die.

Very slowly, the lights fade out on **JUNIOR.** *Upon his vanishing,* **MARY's** *arms are outstretched.*

MARY *resumes initial position, centre stage. Silence. The pace of the following exchange is very slow.*

MARY: Philip.

Pause.

PHILIP: Mary.

Silence.

Happy anniversary.

Pause.

My darling.

Tableau. Fade out. The end.

CLAIRE
A Comedy

Claire premiered at the Blinding Light!! in Vancouver on April 21, 1999, with the following cast:

1	Brian McGugan
2	Laura Jaszcz
3	Joshua Goodstadt
CLAIRE	S. Siobhan McCarthy

Director:	Brian McGugan
Assistant Director:	Trevor Devall
Stage Manager:	Dean Feser
Set Design:	Grant Kanik

CHARACTERS:

1	male, mid-30s, blonde hair, blue eyes
2	female, mid-30s, black hair, black eyes
3	male, early 20s, black hair, black eyes
CLAIRE	10, black hair, black eyes

All of the characters maintain a home position on the stage:

1

2   **3**

CLAIRE

Pool of light on **CLAIRE**, *sitting cross-legged down centre, a bouquet of forget-me-nots in her hands, a baseball bat in her lap, looking unblinkingly into the audience. This light remains fixed on* **CLAIRE** *for most of the play. The stage behind her is dark.*

Voices.

VOICE OF 3: I am no one.

Beat.

VOICE OF 2: I am no one.

Beat.

VOICE OF 1: I am no one.

Light on 3, middle left.

3: [*Matter-of-factly, with a smile.*] He had hair that glistened like the sun, my lover, and eyes as blue as the sky. Cloudless. Every night he would kill me with his eyes, my lover, and everything would fall into place.

Pause.

Had a tiff with him last night. We were just about ready to make love. I wanted to fuck *him*, he was always fucking *me*, but he refused. Flat out refused. Said it was against natural law for *me* to fuck *him*, said he'd sooner eat shit than be the fuck*ee*. So he beat me black and blue and raped me. Rivers of blood from my ass.

Pause.

A few hours later he was asleep. So I grabbed a butcher knife from the kitchen and killed him. Chopped him into a million little pieces.

Pause.

All I wanted to do was feel my dick in his ass. All I wanted to do was love him.

Light on 2, middle right.

2: [*Ibid.*] My husband came home from work. He was such a nice and soft-spoken man. He had thick blonde hair and the bluest eyes I'd ever seen. The blue of the forget-me-nots in my mother's garden.

Pause.

I was living a picket-fence life. Everything under control. He was a natural at that, my husband. Keeping everything under control. He had a way of making things seem right. As if everything had a clear definition. He hurled me down the stairs once and raped me. I dusted myself off and went on.

Pause.

My husband came home from work. Upstairs our five children were dead. I'd put pillows over their faces and smothered them.

Pause.

My husband came home from work. I'd done exactly what he'd asked me to do. I'd watered the plants, scrubbed the floors, removed every dust ball in sight. He came home and dinner was ready. Ready on the dining room table. He sat himself down and ate. Five seconds later he was dead.

Pause.

I'd put cyanide in his mashed potatoes. He was such a nice and soft-spoken man.

Light on 1, up centre.

1: [*Ibid.*] My wife was crazy about baseball bats.

Pause.

She was a fanatic, the cunt, followed the team wherever it went. My first game as an Astro, I homered. Twice. She wouldn't stop screaming, so I fucked her.

Pause.

My wife was crazy about baseball bats. I'd come home from a road trip and we'd make mad, passionate love. "You're a great lover," she'd say. "I'm no fag," I'd say. Then she'd cry on my shoulder and tell me how much she loved me, that she'd die if anything ever happened to me. "I love you, sir," she'd say, "I love you." But I was never sure whether she really meant it. "Do you mean it?" I'd ask. "Yes, sir," she'd say. So I'd grab a bat from the closet and beat her, beat her, and when I'd finish she'd stare at the bat as if it were God. "I'm yours, sir," she'd tell me afterwards, "I'm yours." And we'd roll around in the light, fucking in her blood.

Pause.

But it just couldn't go on, this beauty, this order. And yesterday, yesterday night, it snapped.

Pause.

We'd just finished making love. I was stroking her black hair and looking into her black eyes. "I love you, sir," she said. "Do you mean it?" I asked. "Of course, sir," she said. Sir? SIR?! "Prove it," I said. So she grabbed the bat from the closet and gave it to me. "Beat me," she said, "beat me." And I did, and she laughed the whole way through. "I love you, sir!" she screamed. "I LOVE YOU!" And then it snapped. It finally snapped.

Pause.

I hated her, the cunt, her devotion, politeness, it had to stop, this order, it had to change. So I turned all the lights off, took the bat to her head and beat her till her brains oozed like toothpaste out of her head. When the clock struck twelve she was dead.

Pause.

Our daughter was watching us, a bunch of forget-me-nots in her hands. "We need numbers, sir," she said. "We need names." I swung the bat across her head and killed her.

Pause.

Clear the bases.

Pause.

Burn the stadium.

Pause.

It's over. Everything ... is over.

Pause.

3: I am not my lover's lover.

2: I am not my husband's wife.

1: I am not my daughter's father and my wife is not my wife.

3: I've sewn my ass shut.

2: I've torn my wedding dress to shreds.

3: A is not A.

2: Two times two is not four.

3: I lick myself clean of the wounds he gave me. Wounds from his hands, wounds from his mouth, his hands and his mouth moving over my body, there is no ceiling and there are no more rules, I will be who I want to be, there is no sun.

2: The pain is gone, the pain in my jaw which he broke three times, in the wrists he twisted, in the breasts he chewed open, I will forget about my house, I will disregard ceilings, I will not live for love, there is no sun.

1: My wife is dead, my daughter is dead, I've quit playing baseball and I have no name, I will be who I want to be, there is no sun, I will not live for love, it is over.

Beat.

No pain.

Beat.

No love.

Beat.

3: I am free.

2: I am free.

1: I am free.

Lights out on 1, 2, and 3.

CLAIRE: [*Singing slowly.*] "Twinkle, twinkle, little star,
How I wonder what you are.
Up above the world so high,
Like a diamond in the sky.
Twinkle, twinkle, little star,
How I wonder what you are."

Lights on 1 and 2. The tone is cautious, the pace irregular. For most of this scene they look at each other only from the corners of their eyes.

1: Hi.

Pause.

2: Hi.

Pause.

1: It's dark.

2: Yes.

1: Very.

2: Yes.

Pause.

2: Nice night.

1: Morning.

2: Night.

1: If you like.

Pause.

2: It's cold.

1: Hot.

2: Cold.

1: If you like.

Pause.

Why are you here?

2: I'm going somewhere.

1: Where are you from?

2: Nowhere.

Pause.

Why are *you* here?

1: I'm running away.

2: Where to?

1: Nowhere.

Pause.

1: You have nice hair.

2: What?

1: Such black hair.

2: [*Louder.*] It's not black.

1: It *is*.

2: [*Angrily.*]: It's blonde! Like the sun!

1: If you like.

84

Pause.

2: You look familiar.

1: No I don't.

2: Yes you do.

1: [*Angrily.*] No I don't! I'm a stranger!

Pause.

2: [*Catching herself.*] You're absolutely right.

1: [*Quieter.*] I'm a stranger.

2: You're absolutely right. I have never met you before today.

Pause.

I have never met you before today.

Pause.

1: Can I ... hold you?

2: What?

1: Can I hold you.

2: No.

1: Please.

2: No!

1: [*Grabbing her violently.*] Please!

2: [*Pulling away from him, in terror.*]: Stop it!

Pause.

1: [*Contrite.*] I'm sorry.

2: You're hurting me!

1: [*Letting go, near tears.*] I'm sorry! Please! I didn't mean it! I'm sorry!

Silence.

2: [*Softer.*] You are?

Pause.

1: Yes.

Silence.

2: [*Quiet terror.*] I'm scared.

Pause.

1: [*Quiet terror.*] So am I.

Pause.

1 slowly comes up behind 2, touches her shoulder, holds her gently.

2: What ... what's your name?

1: No names.

2: What?

1: No names.

Silence.

2: Cunt.

Pause.

Cunt.

Pause.

[*Steely determination.*] Your name is Cunt.

Pause.

1: If you like.

Pause.

1 *has turned to look at* **2**.

2: Our eyes can never meet.

1: No?

2: Never.

1: [*Turning away.*] Yes.

Pause.

2: I'm hot.

1: Are you?

2: Yeah.

Pause.

It's the clothes.

Pause.

They're extraneous.

Silence.

Fuck me.

Pause.

I want you to fuck me.

Pause.

1: I'm scared.

Pause.

2: So am I.

Pause.

1 *reflects, then hesitantly takes* **2** *in his arms.*

We are home.

Pause.

Free.

Pause.

1: We are home.

Pause.

Free.

They both tie blindfolds over their eyes. Then they turn to face one another.

2: [*Her hands gently feeling his chest.*] No pain.

Pause.

No love.

Pause.

Gentle.

Pause.

So gentle.

Pause.

1: [*His hands gently feeling her breasts.*] No pain.

Pause.

No love.

Pause.

Gentle.

Pause.

So gentle.

Fade out.

CLAIRE: [*Meekly but with a sense of pride, more to herself than to anyone else.*]

My name is Claire.

Pause.

I am ten years old.

Pause.

My hair is black.

Pause.

And so are my eyes.

Pause.

I shall be good and not cause trouble and do as Daddy has told me.

Pause.

I shall review my multiplication tables. I shall say my prayers.

Pause.

I am Daddy's daughter, now and forever.

Lights on 1 and 3. The tone is cautious, the pace irregular. They look at each other only from the corners of their eyes.

3: What time is it?

1: Huh?

3: What time is it?

1: No time.

3: Pardon?

1: No numbers, no math, no nothing. Understand?

3: Yes. I forgot. Yes.

Pause.

3: Sir?

1: Don't call me sir.

3: Pardon?

1: Don't call me sir.

3: I'm sorry.

1: Don't say that.

3: I'm sorry.

1: You're so fucking polite.

Pause.

[*Unfeelingly.*] Faggot.

Pause.

3: Huh?

Pause.

1: Are you a faggot?

3: Don't call me that.

1: Well, are you?

3: [*Angrily.*] Don't call me that!

Pause.

1: [*Sincerely.*] I'm sorry.

3: [*Ferociously.*]: DON'T CALL ME THAT!!!

1: I'm sorry.

3: [*In tears.*] You hurt me.

1: I'm sorry.

3: You hurt me!

1: [*Touching his shoulder.*] I didn't mean to—

3: [*Pulling away.*] Don't touch me.

1: Just listen.

3: Don't touch me!

Silence.

Faggot.

Pause.

Faggot.

Pause.

[*Gaining confidence.*] Are *you* a faggot?

Pause.

1: If you like.

Pause.

1: You have nice eyes.

3: What?

1: Such black eyes.

3: They're not black.

1: They are.

3: [*Angrily.*] They're blue! Like the sky!

1: If you like.

Pause.

3: Nice night.

1: Morning.

3: Night.

1: If you like.

3: [*Aggressive.*] It's hot.

1: Cold.

3: Hot.

1: If you like.

3: [*Has the upper hand now.*] What's your name?

1: I don't have a name.

3: Well I'll give you a name.

1: If you like.

Pause.

3: Faggot.

Pause.

Faggot.

Pause.

Faggot.

Pause.

1: If you like.

Pause.

3: Our eyes can never meet.

1: Sir?

3: Never.

1: Sir.

3: Now close your eyes.

1 closes his eyes.

Come to me.

1 comes to him.

Kiss me.

1 kisses him.

Turn around.

1 turns around.

Pull your pants down.

1 pulls his pants down.

Relax.

3 hesitates.

[*In utter exultation, almost in tears.*] Oh God. Oh God. Oh God.

Fade out on 1 and 3.

CLAIRE is on her knees, hands clasped.

CLAIRE: [*Solemnly.*] "Our Father, Who art in heaven,
Hallowed be Thy name;
Thy kingdom come, Thy will be done
On earth as it is in heaven.
Give us this day our daily bread
And forgive us our trespasses,
As we forgive those who trespass against us.
And lead us not into temptation,
But deliver us from evil.
For Thine is the kingdom, the power and the glory,
Forever and ever. Amen."

Lights on 2 and 3, who are blindfolded.

3: Faggot's hands how gentle, even as mine are rough.
Hands so tender up and down my chest, down through
my pants and into my crotch. He kneels at my altar,

blindfolds over our eyes, his tongue wraps ribbons, it's an offering. A gift. In him I am God, in him I am free. I smile for the ribbons and for the eyes I don't see.

2: Cunt's hands how gentle down my neck, over my breasts, blindfolds over our eyes so nothing to see. "You're a goddess," I make him say. "The belle of the ball. The cream of the crop. The most beautiful woman in the world." We fuck for *my* pleasure, and for once it is real. He comes; I come. I am free.

Lights out on 2 and 3.

CLAIRE: [*Slowly, carefully.*] Two times one is two.

Beat.

Two times two is four.

Beat.

Two times three is six.

Beat.

Two times four is eight.

Beat; sound of 2 moaning in the dark.

Two times five is ten.

Beat.

Two times six is twelve.

Beat.

Two times seven is fourteen.

Beat.

Two times eight is sixteen.

Beat.

Two times nine is eighteen.

Beat.

Two times ten is ... is ...

Sound of 2 coming, screaming.

Help! Help!

Pause.

Two times one is two.

Beat.

Two times two is four.

Beat.

Two times three is six.

Beat.

Two times four is eight.

Beat; sound of 3 fucking 1.

Two times five is ten.

Beat.

Two times six is twelve.

Beat.

Two times seven is fourteen.

Beat.

Two times eight is sixteen.

Beat.

Two times nine is eighteen.

Beat.

The grunting crescendoes.

Two times ten is ... is ...

The grunting crescendoes.

Two times ten is ... is ...

Sound of 3 coming, screaming.

Help! HELP!

Pause.

Daddy? DADDY? WHERE ARE YOU?

[*Trembling, terrified.*] IT'S SO DARK, DADDY! IT'S SO DARK!

Lights on 1, 2, and 3 in their original places, all blindfolded.

1: It's dark so nothing to see, nothing blonde and nothing blue. In the dark I subvert everything, everything's upside down. I am Cunt; I am Fag; I am free.

Beat.

3: Blindfold over my eyes.

2: And nothing to see.

3: I've sewn my ass shut.

2: I've torn my wedding dress to shreds.

3: A is not A.

2: Two times two is not four.

3: I am free.

2: I am free.

1: I am free.

Lights out on 1, 2, and 3.

CLAIRE: Daddy's eyes how lovely, but they're always filled with tears. At night when I see him crying I beg him to stop, but he can't. Then I start to cry, and he follows me into my room, says he's sorry he upset me and sings me a funny little song. I laugh, he laughs and we wipe away each other's tears. Then we hug and my soul fills with light.

Lights on 1, 2, and 3. They are all wearing blindfolds, all facing the audience, and though they address one another briefly they seem trapped in their own mental spaces.

2: [*To 1.*] What's wrong?

Pause.

1: Nothing.

Pause.

3: [*To 1.*] Something's wrong.

Pause.

1: Nothing's wrong.

Pause.

[*With a smile.*] I had a friend once, a boy. He's dead now. In heaven. He had a father that he loved, that he idolized, so I've heard. Sometimes, so I've heard, he'd fail his father at a baseball game. "Faggot," his father would call him, and he'd make the boy do penance. After the game he'd take him home and drag him to his sister's bedroom. He'd take a gun to the boy's head and tell the poor simp to fuck her. "I'm your father," he'd whisper, "you do as I say, or else you'll never enter the kingdom of God." Choking back tears, the boy did as he was told. "Are you a faggot?" his father'd whisper. "'Cause real men don't cry. Crybabies never enter the kingdom of God."

Pause.

So I've heard.

No smile.

97

Lies.

Pause.

Tears are beautiful.

Pause.

Fuck God.

Silence. 2 and 3 have been listening intently to 1. As if by some ineffable magnetic force, they have both turned to face him. Fade out.

Pause.

CLAIRE: Daddy, don't cry. Wherever you are ... don't cry.

Light on 3, blindfolded.

3: [*With a smile.*] My lover, the old one, a memory of him last night. He's on top of me, my leg a giraffe's neck over his shoulder. "Faggot," he calls me. "You godforsaken faggot." I lie there and take it, I hate it but take it. He won't let me be a man and I hate him for it.

Pause.

[*Smile disappears.*] But somehow ... somehow ... I stroke his blonde hair. The ceiling above is a pleasant shade of grey. His eyes are blue like the sky. Cloudless. Somehow, in spite of everything, I'm smiling.

Pause.

[*The smile returns.*] That was the past. I've butchered the ceiling. Blue eyes worth shit in the dark.

Light on 2, blindfolded.

2: [*With a smile.*] My husband, that bastard, a memory of him last night. He pins me down on the dinner table and rapes me, the bastard, his fist pressed hard on my mouth.

Pause.

"Cunt," he calls me. "Cunt."

Pause.

Cunt.

Pause.

[*Smile disappears.*] Cunt.

Pause.

Somehow, in spite of everything, I'm smiling.

Pause.

[*Smile returns.*] But now, things are different. There is no sun. Forget-me-nots dead in my mother's hands.

Pause.

Forget-me-nots dead in my mother's hands.

Pause.

3: Faggot.

2: Cunt.

3: Faggot.

Beat.

Faggot. I'm on top. That's it. That's all it means. I'm a man now. I don't love him. It's dark so I don't love him.

Beat.

2: It's dark and I can't see him. So I don't love him.

Beat.

3: I can't love him.

Beat.

2: I can't.

Beat.

3: I'm scared.

Beat.

2: I'm scared.

Beat.

CLAIRE: I love you, Daddy. I love you.

Beat.

I'm scared, Daddy. I'm scared.

Lights out on 2 and 3.

Light on 1, blindfolded.

1: [*With a smile.*] It all began with a baseball bat.

Pause.

A family heirloom, this baseball bat. First saw it when I was four years old. My father was the greatest hitter the Astros ever had. Wanted to make sure that I followed in his footsteps. So on my fourth birthday he showed me the baseball bat his father had given to him. He put it in my hands, made me hold it, feel it, said that one day my whole world would depend on it. And from that day on he made baseball my life. Every day without fail at 6:30 in the AM it was off to the park for batting practice. Whenever I'd miss he'd come up to me, smile and whisper "Faggot" twenty-three times into my ear. He had blonde hair and blue eyes like the sky. Cloudless. He was such a nice and soft-spoken man.

Pause.

A family heirloom, this bat. No one loved it more than my mother. One day I was sick and woke up early in the morning when I heard Mom screaming and laughing in the basement.

Pause.

The room was bright with light—Dad was scared as hell of the dark—and he was beating Mom silly with his bat. It was sick. Perverted. But I loved it. Every minute of it. His muscles ... his sweat ... it was beautiful. Divine. Dad saw me watching him, caught me hiding in a little corner. He looked up at me, tried to speak, but fell crying on the floor. His shame ... his pain ... it was beautiful. Divine.

Pause.

It went on for a few more years. Loved it. Every minute of it. But one night it all snapped. There was a power outage and it was dark, so I did it. I did it. Clubbed the letch dead with his bat.

Pause.

[*Beginning to laugh.*] After Mom stopped crying—she cried non-stop until dawn—she came to me and handed me the bat. "Your father's dead," she said. "So it's time you took over. Sir." She called me "*sir.*" She lay on the floor, her hair and eyes as black as shit. "Beat me," she said, "or I'll kill myself." I laughed and turned away, she took a gun and blew her hand off. So I did as I was told, beat the shit out of the old cunt; and Eureka!—the lights flashed back on.

Pause.

[*Becoming increasingly feverish.*] It went on for a few more years. It was sick. Perverted. But I loved it. Every minute of it—the house aglow with light. But one day when I was eighteen everything snapped. For good. I woke up in the middle of the night and finally decided ... I wanted to *see*! So I turned every light in the house off and killed her, killed her, took the bat to her black head and sent her sick soul to heaven. As she took her last breath her eyes melted into mine. "Thank you," she said. And she died.

Pause.

I chopped her up, the old cunt, the way I chopped up Dad, chopped her into a million little pieces. Then I scattered her over the lake, the little lake in the woods, and on the shore bloomed forget-me-nots as blue as my father's eyes.

Pause.

They're dead. They're all dead. But I'm alive. Alive.
Forget-me-nots dead in my daughter's hands.

Pause.

Lights on 2 and 3, blindfolded.

3: It's dark and I can't see him. So I don't love him.

Beat.

I can't love him.

Beat.

2: I can't.

Beat.

CLAIRE: I love you, Daddy. I love you.

Beat.

3: [*To 1, hesitantly.*] I love you.

Beat.

2: [*To 1, hesitantly.*] I love you.

Beat.

CLAIRE: Take me home, Daddy! Take me home!

Beat.

3: Say you love me.

Beat.

2: Say you love me.

Beat. Light out on 1.

CLAIRE: I'm lost. I don't know where I am. Where are you,
Daddy? I miss you! I miss your smile, your blonde hair ...
your beautiful blue eyes.

3: [*No smile.*] Your lips. Your hands. The graceful curve of your body. The only things I know you by. And it's enough.

2: [*Ibid.*] Enough. Your hands so nervous over my neck and down. Even as you fuck me you seem shy. Guilty.

3: [*Ibid.*] You've swallowed your pride—you've let me take over. I use you, defile you, but you never say a word. Is it your hand stroking my hair every time after we fuck? Is there something—*something*—beneath the fear and trembling?

2: [*Ibid.*] You sob into my breast every time after you come. I don't know what to think, I don't know what to feel. All I know is that I'm holding you while I hold onto myself. I want these blindfolds off, I want your looks to kill me; but I clutch onto your head and hold on.

3: [*Ibid.*] I've painted a picture of you in my head. I tried to hold on, I didn't want to do it. But in my mind you have hair that glistens like the sun, and your eyes are blue like the sky. Cloudless.

2: [*Ibid.*] I love the sound of your voice whenever you sing in your sleep. A standard ditty, usually, but such a deep, pleasing voice. You're such a nice and soft-spoken man.

3: [*Ibid.*] When I was a little boy I was scared to death of the dark. Every night I'd scream like crazy when my father turned the lights off. So he'd zoom back to my bedroom and turn the lights back on, and hold me in his arms until I fell asleep.

2: [*Ibid, overlapping 3.*] When I was a little girl I was scared to death of the dark. Every night I'd scream like crazy when my father turned the lights off. So he'd zoom back to my bedroom and turn the lights back on, and hold me in his arms until I fell asleep.

CLAIRE: It's dark, Daddy. It's so dark.

Beat.

3: Give me sun.

Beat.

2: Give me sun.

Beat.

CLAIRE: I'm cold, Daddy. I'm so cold.

Beat.

3: Take me home.

Beat.

2: Take me home.

Beat.

CLAIRE: Daddy? Daddy? You know how scared I am of the dark. Remember how I'd scream when you'd turn the lights off at night? And how you'd run back to me and hug me, and tell me sweetly, "I love you?"

Beat.

2: [*Bitter smile.*] The ceiling above is a pleasant shade of grey. The cuts on my breasts are red gaping mouths. Hot tears slide from my eyes to the bed. Sunlight streams through the blinds.

Beat.

3: [*Bitter smile.*]: The ceiling above is a pleasant shade of grey. My pants and underwear lie torn on the floor. The glass in the mirror breaks and cascades. Sunlight streams through the blinds.

Beat.

2: Blue eyes on me, pin me to the bed.

3: Forget-me-nots in vase, alive and well.

2: [*Taking off blindfold.*] I tried. But I have to see you.

3: I have to see you.

104

Beat.

2: I'm weak. I have to love you.

3: I have to love you.

Light out on 3. Light on 1, with blindfold. An agitated 2, sans blindfold, slowly approaches him.

2: You.

1: Yeah.

2: This isn't enough.

1: Huh?

2: I want to see you.

1: What?

2: [*Grabbing him.*] I *have* to see you.

1: No.

2: [*Desperately.*] Please!

1: No!

2: Please!

1: No!

She tries to remove his blindfold. They struggle.

2: Blue eyes.

1: No.

2: Blue eyes!

1: No!

2: Blue eyes!!

1: No!!

2: Blue eyes!!!

1: No!!!

2 rips off his blindfold.

[*Erupting, seizing her by the throat.*] Do you know what you've done?

2: [*Quailing.*] No!

1: Do you know what this means?

2: Please!

He tries to strangle her. Moments pass before he releases her. She is coughing, her hand on her throat.

1: [*Helplessly, somewhat derisively, shaking his head.*] It's over ... you've ruined it ... it's over ...

Pause.

2 continues to cough.

It's over ... you've ruined it ... it's over ...

Pause.

2's coughs subside. She is looking at him.

2: [*Slowly.*] Blue eyes ... blue eyes ... like the forget-me-nots ... in my mother's garden ...

Pause.

2 rises slowly, 1 moves away from her.

The light. It's come back. It's blinding me. Burning my skin. I hate it. Loved the dark. But light is God. And God is right.

Pause.

Right now, looking at you ... your blonde hair ... your blue eyes ... everything's crumbling ... all my dreams ... everything I wanted to be ...

Pause.

"Though you slay me, yet will I trust you." Daddy always told me to live by God's will. I'm such a sweet and obedient little girl.

Pause.

She advances slowly towards him.

Underneath it all this is what you want, isn't it? My father? My lord? ... *Sir?*

She runs her hands over his chest, speaks firmly.

I know what I've done ... I know what this means.

She strokes his hair.

I love you. It's sick. But I love you.

She kisses his left cheek.

Tell me you love me.

She kisses his right cheek.

Tell me you love me.

She kisses his forehead.

Tell me you love me.

She kisses his lips.

1: [*Hesitating before answering flatly, helplessly, emotionlessly.*] I love you.

They kiss. Lights fade out on them.

CLAIRE: And how I'd wake up in the morning and find you holding me in your arms, a golden thread of sunlight streaming through the blinds?

*Lights on **1** and **3**. They are both wearing blindfolds. **3** is behind **1**, fucking him.*

*Suddenly **3** pulls away from **1**, zips his pants up. Long silence.*

3: [*Finally.*] A *is* A.

Pause.

Two times two *is* four.

Pause.

The ceiling *is* the ceiling.

Pause.

The floor *is* the floor.

Pause.

He laughs bitterly.

I was on a roll for a little while. Almost thought I could pull it off. And then it started happening: the soft feel of your lips ... the passing warmth of your hands ... the sad stories you'd suddenly tell, your voice on the verge of breaking ... And it was all downhill from there—I nearly killed myself last night. It's sick. Perverted. I'm in love.

Pause.

He takes off his blindfold, slowly goes to 1, and gently and sensuously takes off his. They stare at each other for about five seconds.

Well, what do you know. Just as I expected. Blonde hair glistening like the sun.

He runs his hands over 1's chest.

I love you. It's sick. But I love you. You need me as much as I need you.

He kisses 1's left cheek.

You know this is natural. You know this is right.

He kisses 1's right cheek.

Beautiful blue eyes. Like the sky. Cloudless. The bluest blue eyes ... they're blinding me, killing me.

He kisses 1's forehead.

I love you. It's sick. But I love you.

He kisses 1's lips.

Don't worry. I know exactly what this means.

Pause.

Gently and hesitantly, 1 begins to touch 3's face. They kiss passionately.

Fade out.

CLAIRE: Two times one is two.

Beat.

Two times two is four.

Beat.

Two times three is six.

Beat.

Two times four is eight.

Beat; sound of 1 hitting 2 and 2 gasping.

Two times five is ten.

Beat.

Two times six is twelve.

Beat.

Two times seven is fourteen.

Beat.

Two times eight is sixteen.

Beat.

Two times nine is eighteen.

Beat.

Two times ten is ... is ...

VOICE OF 1: It's morning!

VOICE OF 2: Yes!

VOICE OF 1: Morning!

Beat.

VOICE OF 1: It's black!

VOICE OF 2: Yes!

VOICE OF 1: Black!

Sound of 1 hitting 2 one last time.

CLAIRE: [*Ecstatically.*] Twenty! Twenty!! TWENTY!!!

Long pause.

Sound of 1 and 2 breathing heavily.

2: [*Wearily but longingly.*] Give me a name.

Beat.

Give me a name.

Fade out on 1 and 2.

CLAIRE: My name is Claire. My name is Claire. Now and forever. Claire.

Pause.

Two times one *is* two.

Beat.

Two times two *is* four.

Beat.

Two times three *is* six.

Beat.

Two times four *is* eight.

Beat; sound of **1** *fucking* **3**.

Two times five *is* ten.

Beat.

Two times six *is* twelve.

Beat.

Two times seven *is* fourteen.

Beat.

Two times eight *is* sixteen.

Beat.

Two times nine *is* eighteen.

Beat.

Two times ten *is* twenty.

Beat; sound of **1** *and* **3** *coming, screaming.*

Twenty. Twenty. Is. It *is*.

VOICE OF 1: It's morning.

VOICE OF 3: Yes.

VOICE OF 1: Morning.

Beat.

VOICE OF 1: They're black.

VOICE OF 3: Yes.

VOICE OF 1: Black.

Beat.

CLAIRE: Twenty. Twenty. Is. It *is.*

3: [*Wearily but longingly.*] Give me a name.

Beat.

Give me a name.

Beat.

CLAIRE: My name is Claire. My name is Claire. Now and forever. Claire.

CLAIRE speaks very slowly. The light on her is now exceptionally bright.

My name is Claire.

Pause.

I am ten years old.

Pause.

My hair is black.

Pause.

And so are my eyes.

Pause.

I shall be good and not cause trouble and do as Daddy has told me.

Pause.

I shall review my multiplication tables. I shall say my prayers.

Pause.

I am Daddy's daughter—now and forever.

*Light on **1**, in his original position. The stage, formerly dark, is now bright with light.*

1: [*Smiling, eyes glazed.*] It's over. Finished. The cunt and the fag. Shred them into a million little pieces.

Pause.

There is no sun. Two times two is not four. Forget-me-nots dead in my daughter's hands.

Pause.

CLAIRE: Daddy, don't cry. Wherever you are ... don't cry.

Pause.

Remember how I'd see you beating Mommy with your bat? You'd lock yourself in the bathroom, crying like a little baby. Then I'd knock quietly on the door, beg you to let me in, and tell you to stop crying, because nobody's perfect.

Pause.

And remember how you'd beat yourself up with your bat? And how I'd scream at you to stop, that you should beat me instead?

1: [*Ibid.*] There is no sun. Two times two is not four. Forget-me-nots dead in my daughter's hands.

Pause.

The stage continues to brighten.

CLAIRE: Remember that little song you used to sing me every night?

Sings.

"Twinkle, twinkle, little star,
How I wonder what you are."

And remember those mornings when I'd wake up in your arms? "Promise me," you'd whisper, "that you'll never tell Mommy." "I promise," I'd say. It was the least that I could do.

She licks her lips. The next few lines are very slow.

[*With a smile.*] I knew what you were doing. I'm smarter than you think. It was wrong. Sick. And I loved it. Every minute of it.

1: [*Ibid.*] There is no sun. Two times two is not four. Forget-me-nots dead in my daughter's hands.

Pause.

CLAIRE: Your eyes are blue. Your hair is blonde. You're such a nice and soft-spoken man.

CLAIRE rises and slowly turns to face 1. They look at one another intensely for ten seconds, after which CLAIRE begins to slither towards 1. The stage continues to grow ever brighter.

[*Slowly, sounding a bit like Marilyn Monroe.*]

"Twinkle, twinkle, little star,
How I wonder what you are.
Up above the world so high,
Like a diamond in the sky."

The bat upright before her face, she goes down on her knees and begins to lick the bat bottom to top and down again, slowly, lasciviously. Smiling seductively she hands the bat to 1, who hesitates for a few seconds before taking it. CLAIRE slithers closer toward him. Fade out.

CLAIRE's voice in the dark.

[*Very slowly.*] "Twinkle, twinkle, little star,
How I wonder what you are."

Voices in the dark. The last lines are very slow.

VOICE OF 3: I'm alive.

Pause.

VOICE OF 2: I'm alive.

Pause.

VOICE OF CLAIRE: I'm alive.

*Lights on **2, 3,** and **CLAIRE**. The stage is brighter than ever and continues to brighten.*

3: I am Fag.

Pause.

2: I am Cunt.

Pause.

CLAIRE: I am home.

Blinding light. The end.

STAR

A Monologue

Star was given a staged reading at the Asian Heritage Month festival in Vancouver in May 1998, with the following cast:

BROTHER   Josh Haggarty

Director: Brian McGugan

BROTHER, any age

BROTHER in bed.

BROTHER: Kleenex.

Pause.

Linen.

Pause.

Walls and bed milk-white.

Pause.

Silk-smooth teddy polar bear.

Pause.

Tears down cheek like lard.

Pause.

Little sister Myra.

Pause.

Little Miss Miami.

Pause.

Diamonds God-white stars in dark.

Pause.

Dimpled thank-you smile.

Pause.

"Hey, big brother, don't smoke inside the house."

Pause.

Morning eyes bright berry-blue.

Pause.

Star-round tray.

Pause.

Out.

Pause.

"Hey, big brother, give me back my teddy."

Pause.

Morning lips sweet ketchup-red.

Pause.

Snow-cold shower.

Pause.

Stoplight.

Pause.

Moon-kissed scalp, star of gold.

Pause.

Face as mild as cream.

Pause.

Hair like tuft, lemon-light.

Pause.

Stars ablaze mouth-ends.

Pause.

Stars 'round head, gift of wings.

Pause.

Flowers wet with joy.

Pause.

Brother happy, mouth a-drip.

Pause.

Queen afloat throne-bed.

Pause.

Baby queen.

Pause.

Lily queen.

Pause.

Hand silk lace 'round stems.

Pause.

Light through blinds, optic trick.

Pause.

Hand not silk but snake.

Breathing heavily.

Next to you, finger face.

Pause.

Spit down throat like milk.

Pause.

Fingers brown ... down arms ... milk-white ...

Pause.

Snake ... twines ... snake ... night's ... end ...

Comes.

Pause.

From under bed, pulls out box.

Withdraws blonde wig. Wears it.

Diamond tiara. Wears it.

Bouquet of lilies. Holds it.

[*Smiling.*] Sister.

Pause.

Sister.

Pause.

Star o'er high white hill.

Pause.

Tearstained cheeks, baby-white.

Pause.

Hot milk up sweet thighs.

End.

C.E. Gatchalian was born in Vancouver, Canada. He studied Creative Writing and Theatre at the University of British Columbia (BFA, 1996; MFA, 2002). His first play, *Motifs & Repetitions*, aired on Canada's Bravo! channel in 1997 and on the Knowledge Network series *Independent Eye* in 1998. His second play, *Claire*, was produced in Vancouver in 1999. His features and arts criticism have appeared in such publications as *Xtra! West* (to which he is a regular contributor), the *Vancouver Sun*, and the *Georgia Straight*. *Motifs & Repetitions & Other Plays* is his first book.

Bryan Wade is one of Canada's finest playwrights. His plays have been produced by numerous theatre companies across the country, including Factory Theatre Lab, Tarragon Theatre, the Blyth Festival, and Alberta Theatre Projects. Several of his plays have been published by Playwrights Canada Press, including an anthology of five plays called *Blitzkrieg and Other Plays*. He currently teaches playwriting at the University of British Columbia.

The New Hogarth Press is the literary wing of **Zero Summer Productions**, a Vancouver-based collective of artists and writers dedicated to producing and publishing the finest in alternative theatre and literature. It is a division of **The Writers' Collective**, an international association of independent writers and publishers.